HOW TO ALWAYS REAP A HARVEST

HOW TO ALWAYS REAP A HARVEST

Mark T. Barclay

All scripture references are quoted from the
King James Version of the Holy Bible
unless otherwise noted.

First Printing 1994

ISBN 0-944802-12-5

Published by: Mark Barclay Ministries
aka Mark Barclay Publications

Printed in USA

Write:
Mark Barclay Ministries
P.O. Box 588, Midland, MI 48640-0588

Cover Design:
Heart Art & Design
501 George Street, Midland, MI 48640

CONTENTS

INTRODUCTION

In my years of ministry I have watched suffering humanity, and it touches me deeply inside to see so many people tormented and hurting. It is not good that so many are losing the battles and barely weathering the storms of life. It is the will of God that we are triumphant and glorious.

There are so many different realms of life and many different seasons. Of course the most coveted of these is harvesttime. Everyone wants to enjoy harvesttime and have it come more often. We can all reap good things for our lives by simply living according to the rules that govern these things.

In this book I want to explain to you the principles that make men successful and fruitful. You, also, will be able to use these principles to live a better life. The better your life is, the more you can do to serve God and help other people. This is the plan of God.

The things found on these pages are absolutes if you apply them scripturally. They are the words of our Lord, therefore, they will produce for you. God does not choose certain people to bless and others to curse. Get it in your head and heart that God wants **you** blessed, and He will do all He can to get you there.

I will be sharing seven major, yet simple, principles that are all scriptural and very adequate for you to form a lifestyle of productivity. Be sure to memorize them and put them into practice, but always remember that it is the Lord who prospers you.

> *"Beware that thou forget not the* LORD *thy God, in not keeping his commandments, and his judgments, and his statutes, which I command thee this day:*
>
> *Lest when thou hast eaten and art full, and hast built goodly houses, and dwelt therein;*
>
> *And when thy herds and thy flocks multiply, and thy silver and thy gold is multiplied, and all that thou hast is multiplied;*
>
> *Then thine heart be lifted up, and thou forget the* LORD *thy God, which brought thee forth out of the land of Egypt, from the house of bondage . . ."*
>
> Deuteronomy 8:11-14

> *"And thou say in thine heart, My power and the might of mine hand hath gotten me this wealth.*
>
> *But thou shalt remember the* LORD *thy God: for it is he that giveth thee power to get wealth, that he may establish his covenant which he sware unto thy fathers, as it is this day."*
>
> Deuteronomy 8:17-18

BIBLE FACT #1
THE THINGS OF GOD MUST BE SPIRITUALLY DISCERNED

All the things of God must be spiritually discerned. No matter how smart you are or how much you try, you will not figure them out in the natural. Many people cause their own frustration by trying to be close to God and still walk by the flesh. This is impossible.

> *"But the natural man receiveth not the things of the Spirit of God: for they are foolishness unto him: neither can he know them, because they are spiritually discerned."*
>
> 1 Corinthians 2:14

". . . Because they are spiritually discerned." The natural man is losing today because he doesn't know about the things of God. He cannot even recognize them most of the time. In fact, when he is told about them, he considers them nothing but foolishness and fantasy. His mind (which has been programmed and trained in worldly knowledge and worldly ways) functions totally different than a man who has a renewed mind.

A man who has a renewed mind refuses the natural things and lives by the principles of God. We are talking "major differences" here. After a man renews his mind, he begins to understand what God is really saying to him. He begins to prove the will of God in his life.

> *"While we look not at the things which are seen, but at the things which are not seen: for the things which are seen are temporal; but the things which are not seen are eternal."*
>
> 2 Corinthians 4:18

That's right! We must learn to refuse conformity to the world and its ways. This is not easy—especially in the beginning. We have been brought up in worldly philosophies, and we are surrounded with people who live this way.

The answer is not isolation. We cannot run away to a hiding place and never be seen again. No, that's not the answer. Doing this will not make you successful and abundant. Besides, even if you separated yourself from all the people, you would still be stuck with your unrenewed mind.

What shall we do then? Be transformed by the renewing of our mind. The beauty of this is that it is not only available to all of us, but it is the will of God. He will actually help us do this.

You and I won't reap a consistent harvest until we do it God's way. We must begin to think the thoughts of God. Where do we find these thoughts? In the Bible, the Holy Scriptures. Other books will help us and even train us, but only the Bible, the written Word of God, will wash us and renew us.

> *"That he might sanctify and cleanse it with the washing of water by the word . . ."*
>
> Ephesians 5:26

There is no shortcut, and there is no easy way. Nobody can do this for you. It will not come by the laying on of hands, anointing oil, counseling, prophecy, or any other person. It will only happen when you spend time daily in the Word of God.

> *"But if our gospel be hid, it is hid to them that are lost:*
>
> *In whom the god of this world hath blinded the minds of them which believe not, lest the light of the glorious gospel of Christ, who is the image of God, should shine unto them."*
>
> 2 Corinthians 4:3-4

THE THINGS OF GOD ARE SPIRITUALLY DISCERNED. When a person receives Jesus as his or her personal Savior, things begin to change. The old, natural man and his ideas begin to fade away, and a new man gets in position to take charge. A day at a time, the Spirit of God becomes more and more a reality. Through Bible teaching, personal study, and fellowship with those who live these things, a person soon gets a grasp on the things of God.

One more thing. The baptism in the Holy Spirit is a must. You need the presence of the Holy Spirit in your life. He will add to your mind's ability by teaching you, quickening you, and bringing all things to your remembrance.

> *"And I will pray the Father, and he shall give you another Comforter, that he may abide with you for ever;*
>
> *Even the Spirit of truth; whom the world cannot receive, because it seeth him not, neither knoweth him: but ye know him; for he dwelleth with you, and shall be in you."*
>
> John 14:16-17

> *"But the Comforter, which is the Holy Ghost, whom the Father will send in my name, he shall teach you all things, and bring all things to your remembrance, whatsoever I have said unto you."*
>
> John 14:26

Remember, the natural man cannot receive the things of God. In fact, he can't even know them. We just read this in 1 Corinthians 2:14.

My friend, if you don't receive and purpose to adapt to the first chapter of this book, there is no reason to read on. But if you are applying this first chapter to your life, and you are purposing to live accordingly, I have good news for you. Read on.

BIBLE FACT #2
YOU MUST LEARN TO PLANT SPIRITUALLY

Everyone realizes that a harvest only comes after one plants a seed, waters it, and allows it to grow to maturity. Even God normally works by these principles.

> *"Verily, verily, I say unto you, Except a corn of wheat fall into the ground and die, it abideth alone: but if it die, it bringeth forth much fruit."*
>
> John 12:24

> *"Be not deceived; God is not mocked: for whatsoever a man soweth, that shall he also reap.*
>
> *For he that soweth to his flesh shall of the flesh reap corruption; but he that soweth to the Spirit shall of the Spirit reap life everlasting."*
>
> Galatians 6:7-8

Many people are not wise enough to sow in the realm of the spirit. I have found that even people who are good sowers in the natural are not so good spiritually. Sowing in the natural is not the way. It was (and is) meant for a Christian to become spiritually minded.

If a man sows to **his flesh**, he will of the flesh reap

corruption. We just read that. Notice again that he was sowing to "his" flesh. That's the biggest reason it brings corruption. It isn't right to sow to yourself.

Notice also that we are to sow to the Spirit. If we sow to the Spirit and in the realm of the spirit (in other words, do it spiritually), we will reap life. This works in every area of life.

The corruption of the flesh is that it will fade, rust, and eventually pass away. The beauty of the spiritual is that it is eternal. Of course, sowing to the Holy Spirit brings indescribable returns.

There are different spheres of life to sow from and into. You can sow a crop with your money, and you can reap financially as well as heavenly rewards. You can sow from the words of your mouth and reap all kinds of things—both good and bad—according to what you are saying. In fact, every other realm is affected by this sowing of words. (Read James 3:5-6.) You can sow with your possessions and reap a like reward. You can sow your time in servanthood and have it redeemed tremendously as well as have great heavenly rewards.

Sowing means that you are giving or planting something that is yours into someone else. Many people sow generously, but they do it after the world's way and not after God's. It won't work! You must sow spiritually and as unto God—no matter what you are sowing and no matter where you are sowing it.

Where you sow is also very important (I mean to whom and what place). Is it of the flesh or is it of the Lord—the place I mean? The Bible tells us that even our tithe is to be sown properly. Check out these scriptures.

"And it shall be, when thou art come in unto the land which the LORD thy God giveth thee for an inheritance, and possessest it, and dwellest therein;

That thou shalt take of the first of all the fruit of the earth, which thou shalt bring of thy land that the LORD thy God giveth thee, and shalt put it in a basket, and shalt go unto the place which the LORD thy God shall choose to place his name there."

Deuteronomy 26:1-2

"He that hath pity upon the poor lendeth unto the LORD; and that which he hath given will he pay him again."

Proverbs 19:17

"Give, and it shall be given unto you; good measure, pressed down, and shaken together, and running over, shall men give into your bosom. For with the same measure that ye mete withal it shall be measured to you again."

Luke 6:38

Giving is a beautiful thing all by itself. But the great return meant for you by God will be hindered if you sow with the wrong attitude, in the wrong way, with the wrong motive, for the wrong results, or to the wrong places.

Sowing to yourself is not permitted and will only ruin your life. The same is true with sowing in the realm of the flesh or in fleshly ways.

You must be spiritual and sow all your seed, no matter the kind, into the realm of the spirit and with the help of the Holy Spirit. It must be planted spiritually.

BIBLE FACT #3
GET IT INTO SEED FORM

Don't discredit this fact as being unwise or less important. Many people who give into others are simply scattering their goods. If you want to be a precise sower and an abundant reaper, then you will have to learn to break things down. Let me explain this a little further.

> *"If ye have faith as a grain of mustard seed, ye shall say unto this mountain, Remove hence to yonder place; and it shall remove: and nothing shall be impossible unto you."*
>
> Matthew 17:20

Please note here that Jesus was telling us to have faith "as" a seed—not a seed but **as** a seed. The subject here is not so much mustard seed as it is the life process of the seed. He also taught about planting it and watching it grow into a huge plant for harvest.

> *"It is like a grain of mustard seed, which, when it is sown in the earth, is less than all the seeds that be in the earth:*
>
> *But when it is sown, it groweth up, and becometh greater than all herbs, and shooteth out great branches; so that the fowls of the air may lodge under the shadow of it."*
>
> Mark 4:31-32

For years I thought Jesus was telling them about little faith. I really thought He was getting after them because of the "size" of their faith. One day as I was meditating on this, I was inspired to compare these scriptures above. I realized then that it wasn't the size that Jesus was dealing with but the way the process works.

It isn't that you need little or big faith. It's most important that you know to plant it as a seed. Even if your faith is small, get it into seed form, plant it spiritually, and it will grow. Get it into seed form! This was Jesus' explanation to His disciples when He was explaining their power level. It wasn't so much a lack of faith but a misuse of it.

Take what faith you do have (even if it's just a measure) sow it into a spiritual project, and watch it grow.

This was me. I had mustard seed faith. It fell way short of what was needed to get the job done. But just like the little mustard seed (the smallest of all other seeds), when it was properly planted, it grew into a great plant. This doesn't happen overnight. It wasn't instant harvest-time.

It took days upon days for my faith to grow. It took planting after planting to keep full rows of healthy crops in every field of my life. Even today, I have learned that the moment I reap a harvest, I must take some of the seed and replant my field. If I devour all the seed that I reap during harvest, I have nothing to replant my field with; thus this area of my life will be barren during the next harvest season.

Planting seeds that others give you is also very important. Many people blow it right here. Let me share with you how I began to learn this.

Vickie and I made it a point to be at every major convention or camp meeting where the uncompromised Word was being taught. (We still are so hungry for the truth.) We would sit in those meetings, take notes, mark our Bibles, and just be saturated with the truth.

Even so, I found myself doing something that was causing great frustration in our lives. I was imitating those great teachers so much that I was beginning to sound like them.

I would sit in those meetings and listen to the testimonies of how their great faith brought them such good results. They would tell us how they believed for great things and got them. I got all fired up and went out to do the same thing.

I began to be disappointed because I was not getting the same results. My testimony was far from what I heard in these conventions. It really began to bother me that it would work for others but not me.

Follow closely now. I knew that what those great men of God were teaching was the gospel truth. **Yet it wasn't working for me.** This caused me to go through different phases and stages of the flesh.

First I wanted to say that these things only work for great men and not for everyday people like me; but I discovered that God doesn't work that way. Then I began to condemn myself because I was sure that I wasn't worth anything, that my faith was way too small, and that God was never going to use me. Get the picture?

As I sought the Lord on this, he revealed to me a very simple—yet life-changing—truth. The Lord showed me to get it into seed form. That's right—get it into seed form. Let me explain.

All those great men of God were testifying and sharing how they planted seed and now were receiving great blessings. I got so excited about airplanes, buildings, cars, and miracles that I got my eyes off the principles being taught. Those great Bible teachers were telling me about **their** harvesttimes, not mine.

They were taking a portion of their well-deserved, newly-harvested crop and putting some seed back into the ground. They were nice enough to sow some of their seed from the harvest into my life. When I realized I could take that testimony (that seed) and plant it in my own life, it grew for me just like it did for them.

You see, it was their harvest, not mine. It was their harvest, and they were giving me some of that prime seed that I might plant it also. All I had to do was take that seed and plant it.

Do you understand? It wasn't my harvest, it was theirs. Their harvest testimony was now my seed. If planted properly, it would produce after its own kind. This is the law of God.

BIBLE FACT #4
SEEDTIME AND HARVEST

"And he said, So is the kingdom of God, as if a man should cast seed into the ground;

And should sleep, and rise night and day, and the seed should spring and grow up, he knoweth not how.

For the earth bringeth forth fruit of herself; first the blade, then the ear, after that the full corn in the ear.

But when the fruit is brought forth, immediately he putteth in the sickle, because the harvest is come."

Mark 4:26-29

This passage of scripture is almost self-explanatory. Jesus is expounding with clarity just how the kingdom of God works. This has been a long-sought-after truth. The amazing thing is that it has been right here in the Bible all these years. Let's look a little closer.

1. Jesus explained that the kingdom of God is similar to a man planting seed into the ground.

2. Then Jesus began to explain how this man was to act while his seed was out of sight (in the ground). He was to leave that seed alone until it sprang up and grew into a plant. What was he to do during this

process? Sleep and rise, night and day. This tells me that he wasn't concerned with the seed that he planted. It also shows us that he didn't necessarily know how all this was going to work. He just had simple faith that the planted seed was going to produce.

3. Jesus continued to reveal to His disciples the way that the Kingdom was built. He explained how the earth brought fruit of herself in its proper stages: first the blade, then the ear, after that the full corn in the ear (a super lesson for us to learn).

4. Jesus even explains here when to harvest. Beware because this is also what the devil waits for. He hovers around you at harvesttime and tries to devour all the seed that you put back into the ground.

When people only have a little bit, they watch it very closely. The devil senses this guard. But when they have much, such as at harvesttime, they tend to get a little less protective because of the abundance.

Jesus told His disciples that they should thrust in the sickle and reap immediately when the fruit was present on the vine. Many believers don't know how to do this. They forget what they have planted where. They don't recognize their harvest when it comes because they have no memory of what is coming.

Study and meditate more on these passages of scripture until they are very clear to you and you can easily apply them to your life.

BIBLE FACT #5
THE PROCESS WILL NEVER CEASE

In the last chapter we discussed how the kingdom of God functions as Jesus explained it to His disciples. He showed us that everything in the Kingdom worked by seed-time and harvest. This process of life is still in operation today. Those who have an understanding of it will be very successful and productive in the things of God.

How do I know that this process is still the same today? Because the Bible very clearly says it is.

> *"While the earth remaineth, seedtime and harvest, and cold and heat, and summer and winter, and day and night shall not cease."*
>
> Genesis 8:22

"While the earth remaineth . . . [it] shall not cease." This is still in effect today. It helps to know this so that you have an understanding of how it all works. Many people sow, but as they do (or directly after), they want to help with the increase. Only God can bring the increase. The ground has an ability in it to bring forth the fruit of the seed. You don't have to help it grow.

The system of sowing in God's kingdom is similar. All we have to do is sow the right seed in the right place in the right way, and the spiritual ground will bring forth fruit of itself. It's a God-created process.

For everything under the sun, there is a season: a time to sow, a time to water, and a time to reap. Just like the natural year has seasons in it—winter, spring, summer, fall—so the spiritual realm has seasons of its own (not the same as natural, worldly ones but of supernatural timing of God).

> *"To every thing there is a season, and a time to every purpose under the heaven:*
>
> *A time to be born, and a time to die; a time to plant, and a time to pluck up that which is planted . . ."*
>
> Ecclesiastes 3:1-2

Nobody sows seed without reaping in mind. The whole idea behind planting is growing a plant. The whole thing behind growing a plant is watching it bear fruit. The whole thing behind watching it bear fruit is harvesting that same fruit. It's as sure as the Word of God—at least as long as the earth remains.

BIBLE FACT #6
JESUS WILL GIVE YOU THE SEED

Jesus will give you seed, look to Him. The Lord Himself will give you the increase (the harvest), and from it, of course, you will have gained plenty of seeds for resowing. If you are just starting out, look to the Lord; for it is He who gives you power to get wealth. He will give you the seed.

> *"But this I say, He which soweth sparingly shall reap also sparingly; and he which soweth bountifully shall reap also bountifully.*
>
> *Every man according as he purposeth in his heart, so let him give; not grudgingly, or of necessity: for God loveth a cheerful giver.*
>
> *And God is able to make all grace abound toward you; that ye, always having all sufficiency in all things, may abound to every good work:*
>
> *(As it is written, He hath dispersed abroad; he hath given to the poor: his righteousness remaineth for ever.*
>
> *Now he that ministereth seed to the sower both minister bread for your food, and multiply your seed sown, and increase the fruits of your righteousness;)"*
>
> 2 Corinthians 9:6-10

First of all, this verse refers to the size of your gift and how frequently it is sown. You can sow sparingly or bountifully. Sparingly means seldom and of smaller percentages of your income. Bountifully means often and a larger portion of your income.

Also note that it is with the heart that man sows. We get to purpose within ourselves what, how often, and to whom we sow. This of course has all to do with your return, so learn to purpose properly.

God is able to cause you to have all sufficiency in all things, and it is His will to do so. If you are a cheerful giver, the Lord loves you.

> *"Now he that ministereth seed to the sower both minister bread for your food, and multiply your seed sown, and increase the fruits of your righteousness . . ."*
>
> 2 Corinthians 9:10

1. Sow bountifully (large amounts and often), and you have a bountiful (large amounts and often) harvest. The more seed in the ground, the more plants you have growing. The more plants you have growing, the more fruit will bear forth. The more fruit that bears forth, the larger the harvest.

2. We can determine how much we sow. We purpose in our hearts to sow any amount, any way, and to anybody we want.

3. Realize that it isn't just the amount of sowing that counts, but the attitude of the sower. We need to be sure we are giving cheerfully and not grudgingly or out of necessity.

4. We will abound to every good work because God Himself is fertilizing the crops. He is assuring a harvest by giving us both His grace in this area and also performing the doing of His Word.

5. Learn that with every harvest and blessing that you tithe first, then sow for a new crop, and then live off the rest. Remember the tithe is not yours, it is the Lord's. You can't consider tithing the same as sowing because you can't claim credit for sowing something that isn't yours.

> *"And all the tithe of the land, whether of the seed of the land, or of the fruit of the tree, is the LORD'S: it is holy unto the LORD.*
>
> *And if a man will at all redeem ought of his tithes, he shall add thereto the fifth part thereof."*
>
> Leviticus 27:30-31

JESUS WILL GIVE YOU THE SEED. If you obey the rules, you will be in a place where Jesus will be able to supply for you and help you meet your needs. The Apostle Paul wrote to the Philippian church that Jesus was going to take care of them according to His riches in glory—because they had sown into his ministry.

The supernatural, heavenly supply comes when you sow into the minister and his ministry.

> *"Now ye Philippians know also, that in the beginning of the gospel, when I departed from Macedonia, no church communicated with me as concerning giving and receiving, but ye only.*
>
> *For even in Thessalonica ye sent once and again unto my necessity.*

Not because I desire a gift: but I desire fruit that may abound to your account.

But I have all, and abound: I am full, having received of Epaphroditus the things which were sent from you, an odour of a sweet smell, a sacrifice acceptable, wellpleasing to God.

But my God shall supply all your need according to his riches in glory by Christ Jesus."

Philippians 4:15-19

BIBLE FACT #7
DON'T SOW DIVERS SEEDS

This just could be the most important thing I have written in this book. You can practice everything I've told you thus far, but if you are sloppy in this area, it will cost you all.

DO NOT SOW DIVERS SEEDS IN YOUR VINEYARD. It will absolutely pervert and defile both your seed sown and your entire system of sowing. In fact, it will literally delete your harvest and spoil your life.

Meditate long on this scripture below until you get it into your entire thinking process and, of course, in your spirit.

> *"Thou shalt not sow thy vineyard with divers seeds: lest the fruit of thy seed which thou hast sown, and the fruit of thy vineyard, be defiled."*
>
> Deuteronomy 22:9

This is exactly where most people ruin it. This is the element that causes them to go shipwreck in more than one area. It certainly fits finances but also covers every sphere of life.

It deals mostly with the words of our mouth. It is the

words of our mouth that justify us and condemn us. Jesus taught that a man is defiled not by what goes into his mouth but by what comes out of it. James taught that a man's whole natural course is directed by the words of his mouth. Check out these scriptures.

> *"For by thy words thou shalt be justified, and by thy words thou shalt be condemned."*
>
> Matthew 12:37

> *"Not that which goeth into the mouth defileth a man; but that which cometh out of the mouth, this defileth a man."*
>
> Matthew 15:11

> *"And the tongue is a fire, a world of iniquity: so is the tongue among our members, that it defileth the whole body, and setteth on fire the course of nature; and it is set on fire of hell."*
>
> James 3:6

> *"Be not deceived; God is not mocked: for whatsoever a man soweth, that shall he also reap."*
>
> Galatians 6:7

> *"Death and life are in the power of the tongue: and they that love it shall eat the fruit thereof."*
>
> Proverbs 18:21

Notice here that there is much reference to your mouth and how it is used. It is no mistake that God is trying to make it very clear to us that we are to put a guard on it. Your vineyard (life or heart) can be totally ruined by your own mouth. You can literally spoil all of your harvest by misusing your mouth.

This is true for every one of us. There is no exception

to this rule. It is absolutely true. Some say, "I don't believe that." I tell you to look at what is happening right now in your life, and it is in direct relation to what you said yesterday or last week or last year.

We forget that we reap what we sow. We sow things today and forget about them months from now. Any good farmer knows that you don't reap in the same day you sow. It takes a while for the crop to come up. The devil likes to be sure that you reap from your bad seed at unexpected times, especially during good times.

Even tithing is in direct relation with your words. The biggest part of tithing is the use of your mouth, and the quickest way to devastate the blessings of the tithe is to misuse your mouth. Check out these scriptures.

> *"And it shall be, when thou art come in unto the land which the LORD thy God giveth thee for an inheritance, and possessest it, and dwellest therein;*
>
> *That thou shalt take of the first of all the fruit of the earth, which thou shalt bring of thy land that the LORD thy God giveth thee, and shalt put it in a basket, and shalt go unto the place which the LORD thy God shall choose to place his name there.*
>
> *And thou shalt go unto the priest that shall be in those days, and say unto him, I profess this day unto the LORD thy God . . ."*
>
> Deuteronomy 26:1-3
>
> *"And thou shalt speak and say before the LORD thy God . . ."*
>
> Deuteronomy 26:5
>
> *"Bring ye all the tithes into the storehouse, that there may be meat in mine house, and prove me now here-*

with, saith the LORD of hosts, if I will not open you the windows of heaven, and pour you out a blessing, that there shall not be room enough to receive it.

And I will rebuke the devourer for your sakes, and he shall not destroy the fruits of your ground; neither shall your vine cast her fruit before the time in the field, saith the LORD of hosts.

And all nations shall call you blessed: for ye shall be a delightsome land, saith the LORD of hosts.

Your words have been stout against me, saith the LORD. Yet ye say, What have we spoken so much against thee?

Ye have said, It is vain to serve God: and what profit is it that we have kept his ordinance, and that we have walked mournfully before the LORD of hosts?"

Malachi 3:10-14

Sowing divers seeds also has to do with where and how you plant your money. It has to do with the friends you have and who you fellowship with. It also has to do with the church you attend and what ministry you are partners with. You have seeds in the form of your words, money, time, relationships, actions, responses, and possessions. Really, every area of your life is affected by this.

You and I will give a severe account to Jesus on Judgment Day for the misuse of these things. You see this over and over again in the teachings of Jesus and Paul. Not only can you hurt your life here on the earth but also taint your day of rewards in Heaven.

Study these things out in their entirety and make the necessary adjustments in your life—TODAY!

CONCLUSION

Isn't the Word of the Lord wonderful? It is not only good to the hearing, but it is so beneficial. Not only does it wash your mind, but it shines light on your path. It feeds your heart with faith. It is healing to your flesh, and when hid in your heart, it will keep you out of sin.

This book was designed to orientate you to the sowing system in God's kingdom. These things will work for you in areas other than money. They will work in money systems, but they are not limited to them.

Be very consistent to use these principles scripturally, and they will guide you from poverty into the beautiful freedom of prosperity. It is God's plan for you to flourish in every area of your life—and you will. Be a wise, generous sower.

FINANCIAL SOWING CHART

1. You must learn to be a giver. It will come back to you.

"Give, and it shall be given unto you; good measure, pressed down, and shaken together, and running over, shall men give into your bosom. For with the same measure that ye mete withal it shall be measured to you again."

Luke 6:38

2. Your return will come as you meet two Bible conditions:

   - Cast your bread on every wave.
   - After many days it will come back to you.

   "Cast thy bread upon the waters: for thou shalt find it after many days."

   Ecclesiastes 11:1

3. Your progress will be hindered as a good spiritual farmer if you look at situations or reasons why you shouldn't give and receive.

   "He that observeth the wind shall not sow; and he that regardeth the clouds shall not reap."

   Ecclesiastes 11:4

4. Your harvest amount depends on the amount you give. You purpose in your heart what you will reap by the amount you sow.

   "But this I say, He which soweth sparingly shall reap also sparingly; and he which soweth bountifully shall reap also bountifully.

   Every man according as he purposeth in his heart, so let him give; not grudgingly, or of necessity: for God loveth a cheerful giver."

   2 Corinthians 9:6-7

5. The words of your mouth can ruin your already planted seed and stop the blessing of the Lord upon your fields.

   "Your words have been stout against me, saith the LORD. *Yet ye say, What have we spoken so much against thee?*

Ye have said, It is vain to serve God: and what profit is it that we have kept his ordinance, and that we have walked mournfully before the LORD of hosts?"

Malachi 3:13-14

6. Be wise where you sow your seed. Whatever field you put it in is the field you'll reap it in. You are the sower. Sow in good ground according to the instructions found in your Bible.

   "Be not deceived; God is not mocked: for whatsoever a man soweth, that shall he also reap.

   For he that soweth to his flesh shall of the flesh reap corruption; but he that soweth to the Spirit shall of the Spirit reap life everlasting." Galatians 6:7-8

7. You must be very, very consistent in giving and confessing. You will reap much if you don't grow tired or faint.

   "And let us not be weary in well doing: for in due season we shall reap, if we faint not." Galatians 6:9

8. Tithing is not the same as giving. Tithing is presenting back to God what is already His. Giving is offering some of what is yours. Giving will determine the amount you harvest, but tithing will protect it until harvest day.

   - Tithing insures your return.
   - It is like an insurance policy.
   - The devourer is rebuked for you.
   - Your fruit will not be destroyed.

"And I will rebuke the devourer for your sakes, and he shall not destroy the fruits of your ground; neither shall your vine cast her fruit before the time in the field, saith the LORD of hosts."

Malachi 3:11

9. Giving to the gospel will give you a hundredfold return in this lifetime.

"And Jesus answered and said, Verily I say unto you, There is no man that hath left house, or brethren, or sisters, or father, or mother, or wife, or children, or lands, for my sake, and the gospel's,

But he shall receive an hundredfold now in this time, houses, and brethren, and sisters, and mothers, and children, and lands, with persecutions; and in the world to come eternal life."

Mark 10:29-30

10. Giving to the poor is like lending to the Lord. He will repay you in perfect time. It is a perfect investment with no risks.

"He that hath pity upon the poor lendeth unto the LORD; and that which he hath given will he pay him again."

Proverbs 19:17

11. Offerings are made to ministries to help pay for buildings and to make sanctuaries where people can come worship the Lord. There are many different reasons to give offerings to the different ministries.

"And the LORD spake unto Moses, saying,

Speak unto the children of Israel, that they bring me an offering: of every man that giveth it willingly with his heart ye shall take my offering."

Exodus 25:1-2

"And they received of Moses all the offering, which the children of Israel had brought for the work of the service of the sanctuary, to make it withal. And they brought yet unto him free offerings every morning.

And all the wise men, that wrought all the work of the sanctuary, came every man from his work which they made;

And they spake unto Moses, saying, The people bring much more than enough for the service of the work, which the LORD commanded to make.

And Moses gave commandment, and they caused it to be proclaimed throughout the camp, saying, Let neither man nor woman make any more work for the offering of the sanctuary. So the people were restrained from bringing.

For the stuff they had was sufficient for all the work to make it, and too much."

Exodus 36:3-7

PRAYER OF SALVATION

YOU CAN BE SAVED FROM ETERNAL DAMNATION and get God's help now in this life. All you have to do is humble your heart, believe in Christ's work at Calvary for you, and pray the prayer below.

"Dear Heavenly Father:

I know that I have sinned and fallen short of Your expectations of me. I have come to realize that I cannot run my own life. I do not want to continue the way I've been living, neither do I want to face an eternity of torment and damnation.

I know that the wages of sin is death, but I can be spared from this through the gift of the Lord Jesus Christ. I believe that He died for me, and I receive His provision now. I will not be ashamed of Him, and I will tell all my friends and family members that I have made this wonderful decision.

Dear Lord Jesus:

Come into my heart now and live in me and be my Savior, Master, and Lord. I will do my very best to chase after You and to learn Your ways by submitting to a pastor, reading my Bible, going to a church that preaches about **You**, and keeping sin out of my life.

I also ask You to give me the power to be healed from any sickness and disease and to deliver me from those things that have me bound.

I love You and thank You for having me, and I am eagerly looking forward to a long, beautiful relationship with You."

Books by Mark T. Barclay

Beware of Seducing Spirits

This is not a book on demonology. It is a book about the misbehavior of men and women and the seducing/deceiving spirits that influence them to do what they do. Brother Barclay exposes the most prominent seducing spirits of the last days.

Building a Supernatural Church

A guide to pioneering, organizing, and establishing a new local church. This is a fast-reading, simple, instructional guide to leaders and helps people who are working together to build the Church.

Charging the Year 2000

This book will remind you of the last-days' promises of God as well as alert you to the many snares and falsehoods with which Satan will try to deceive and seduce last-days' believers. "A handbook for living in the '90s."

Enduring Hardness

God has called His Church an army and the believers, soldiers. It is mandatory that all Christians endure hardness as good soldiers of Jesus Christ. This book will help build more backbone in you.

How to Avoid Shipwreck

A book of preventive medicine, helping people stay strong and full of faith. You will be strengthened by this book as you learn how to anchor your soul.

How to Relate to Your Pastor

It is very important in these last days that God's people understand the office of pastor. As we put into practice these principles, the Church will grow in numbers and also increase its vision for the world.

How to Always Reap a Harvest

In this book Brother Barclay explains the principles that make men successful and fruitful. It shows you how to live a better life and become far more productive and enjoy a full harvest.

Improving Your Performance

Every Christian everywhere needs to read this book. Even leaders will be challenged by this writing. It will help tremendously in the organization and unity of your ministry and working force.

Preachers of Righteousness

This is not a book for pulpiteers or reverends only but for all of us. It reveals the real ministry style of Jesus Christ and the sold-out commitment of His followers—the most powerful, awesome force on the face of the earth.

The Real Truth About Tithing

With the extremely fast lifestyles of these last days, it leaves little time to thoroughly study God's Word. When you finish this book, you will be fully equipped and informed to tithe properly and accurately. All of your tithing questions should be answered. Your life will never be the same.

Sheep, Goats, Wolves

A scriptural yet practical explanation of human behavior in our local churches and how church leaders and members can deal with each other. You will especially enjoy the tests that are in the back of this book.

The Sin of Familiarity

This book is a scriptural study on the most devastating sin in the body of Christ today. The truths in this book will make you aware of this excess familiarity and reveal to you some counterattacks.

The Sin of Lawlessness

Lawlessness always challenges authority and ultimately is designed to hurt people. This book will convict those who are in lawlessness and warn those who could be future victims. It will help your life and straighten your walk with Him.

The Making of a Man of God

In this book you'll find some of the greatest, yet simplest, insights to becoming a man or woman of God and to launching your ministry with accuracy and credibility. The longevity of your ministry will be enhanced by the truths herein. You will learn the difference between being a convert, an epistle, a disciple, and a minister.

The Remnant

God has always had a people and will always have a people. Brother Barclay speaks of the upcoming revival and how we can be those who are alive and remain when our Master returns.

The Captain's Mantle (minibook)

Something happened in the cave Adullum. Find out how 400 distressed, indebted, and discontented men came out of that cave as one of the most awesome armies in history.

Basic Christian Handbook (minibook)

This book contains basic doctrines that are simple yet necessary to every Christian's walk with God. It will be a vital help to new converts in the Kingdom. This also makes a great tract or altar counselor's tool.